FREED FOR DEVOTION

A Carer's Book of Prayers

by

GODFREY H. HOLMES

Foreword by Rev. Margaret Cundiff

Cover illustration by Andrea Grealy

MOORLEY'S Print & Publishing

© Copyright 1999

All rights reserved. No part of this publication may be
reproduced, stored in a retrieval system, or
transmitted, in any form or by any means,
electronic, mechanical, photocopying, recording
or otherwise, without the prior
written permission of the publishers.

British Library Cataloguing in Publication Data.
A catalogue record for this book is available
from the British Library.

ISBN 0 86071 536 1

MOORLEY'S Print & Publishing
23 Park Rd., Ilkeston, Derbys DE7 5DA
Tel/Fax: (0115) 932 0643

DEDICATED

TO

M. M.

District Nurse
Neighbour
Friend

By the same author:-

Truancy & Social Welfare
Bells Ringing In The Distance
Published by Boys' & Girls' Welfare Society.

Alcohol Among Young People
Obtaining The Full Measure
Published by Boys' & Girls' Welfare Society.

Beginning Where I Am:
Meditations For Young People
Published by S.P.C.K. Triangle.

Your Conversation – Or Mine?
200 Tactics When Talking
Published by Nethermoor Books, 1999.

CONTENTS

FOREWORD by Rev. Margaret Cundiff 9

INTRODUCTION 11

HOW TO USE THESE PRAYERS 13

SECTION ONE
UNDERSTANDING
1) A new role in life 17
2) Duty 17
3) Understanding sickness 18
4) Understanding disability 19
5) Understanding old age 19
6) Understanding mental health 20
7) The National Health Service 20
8) Victims or survivors? 21
9) Suicide and attempted suicide 21
10) Caring: paid or unpaid? 22

SECTION TWO
SCURRYING
11) Too busy to think 23
12) Many buckets and bowls 23
13) Many errands 24
14) Many people to consult 24
15) Trying to run a household 25
16) Working late to-night 25
17) Bringing up children as well 26
18) A baby with only a little time to live 26
19) Caring before going to school 27
20) Caring after a full day at work 27

SECTION THREE
SHIELDING
21) Not mentioning myself 29
22) Not talking about the illness 29
23) Not taking all responsibility from other people 30
24) Not challenging when people talk down to me 30
25) Not arguing with the person(s) I am caring for 31
26) Not doing everything 31

27)	Not pressurising the person(s) I am caring for 32
28)	Not correcting 32
29)	Not forbidding 33
30)	Not resigning 33

SECTION FOUR
ADVISING

31)	Give me the right advice to pass on 35
32)	Give me all knowledge about benefits 35
33)	Help me to negotiate 36
34)	Directing someone somewhere else 36
35)	Seeing my advice ignored 37
36)	Seeing my advice overruled 37
37)	Pushing 38
38)	Pulling 38
39)	Tired of the telephone 39
40)	Tired of giving out advice 39

SECTION FIVE
BEFRIENDING

41)	Befriending the prisoner 41
42)	Befriending the drunkard 41
43)	Befriending homeless people 42
44)	Befriending widows and widowers 43
45)	Befriending teenagers 43
46)	Befriending families at risk 44
47)	Befriending women enduring domestic violence 45
48)	Befriending parents who mistreat their children 45
49)	Befriending those who inflict self-harm 46
50)	Befriending complete strangers 46

SECTION SIX
SHARING

51)	I want to donate more to charity 47
52)	I want to give something else 47
53)	I'm thinking of opening my home to ageing parent(s) 48
54)	I want to share my spare time 48
55)	I want to foster 49
56)	I want to adopt 49
57)	I want to marry someone with a disability 50
58)	I want to share caring with the rest of my family 50
59)	I want to share my faith 51
60)	I want to share my optimism 51

SECTION SEVEN
VISITING
- 61) Visiting hospital.. 53
- 62) Visiting special school.. 53
- 63) Visiting a hostel.. 54
- 64) Visiting a hospice 55
- 65) Visiting a children's home 55
- 66) Visiting someone who is very depressed.. 56
- 67) Visiting someone who has had an accident 56
- 68) Visiting someone bereaved.. 57
- 69) Visiting someone who has been burgled 57
- 70) Visiting someone who has recently relinquished caring................ 58

SECTION EIGHT
PRAYING TOGETHER
- 71) A prayer for healing.. 59
- 72) Helping each other... 59
- 73) Seeing a goal 60
- 74) Finding a way out of darkness 60
- 75) Exchanging parent and child roles.. 61
- 76) Looking for new pleasures 61
- 77) A prayer for the rest of this family 62
- 78) A prayer for our neighbours 62
- 79) Thank you for togetherness 63
- 80) Preparing to part 63

SECTION NINE
LOOKING AROUND
- 81) A prayer for other carers... 65
- 82) A prayer for people with no caring responsibilities....................... 65
- 83) A prayer for those employed as social workers 66
- 84) A prayer for occupational therapists... 66
- 85) Praying for a carer's partner... 67
- 86) Looking for new methods of caring 67
- 87) Looking for a permanent solution to suffering 68
- 88) Looking for alternative medicines, alternative treatments............. 68
- 89) Looking for what is sanity or insanity 69
- 90) Looking at developing nations which cannot afford carers 69

7

SECTION TEN
LOOKING FORWARD
- 91) A new sense of purpose 71
- 92) A new person to care for 71
- 93) A new care setting 72
- 94) A new group of colleagues 72
- 95) A New Year of caring 73
- 96) Waiting for more information 73
- 97) Waiting for new inspiration 74
- 98) Waiting for verification 74
- 99) Waiting for marching orders 75
- 100) Waiting for morning 75

CONCLUSION 77

SUGGESTIONS FOR FURTHER READING 79

CONTACT POINTS 81

FOREWORD
By Revd. Margaret Cundiff
Christian Author and Broadcasting Officer
for the Diocese of York.

Being a carer can be a delight, a duty, and a drudgery. Many carers have to hold down a full– or part-time job as well as caring for someone else. Others are very restricted by the needs of the person(s) they care for – which means giving up work, friends, hobbies, or interests in the name of flexibility.

It is "a labour of love," of "hard labour" – or some point in between. Being a carer is always time consuming. There is always someone to consider, to worry about. Then there is the sadness of seeing a loved one getting frailer – often in pain – acting out of character, resentful, even angry about having to be a cared for. Guilt also enters in: the guilt of dependency.

Not easy, having to rely on others for everything, as well as being disabled, ill, elderly – or all three. Especially when you are leaving aside what was such a full and interesting life, able to do what you want, when you want. There used to be choice: the choice to go one way or a different way. Dependency, indeed interdependency, necessarily restricts choice.

For carers, and for friends and relatives cared for, there will be times of anxiety and disagreement. Being in each other's company for so much of each day gives rise to a hidden wish to live on your own again, back in control.

Yet there is also real joy being able to care for somebody you love and cherish. Time together is precious, particularly when you know that time is limited. Blessings and compensations come from that special relationship, however it started. Most times, there is a blood tie; but equally past friendship, or employment, or even holidaying, can have brought two people together at the moment of greatest need.

We all need to share our feelings and thoughts, to draw strength, to receive guidance, to express gratitude, or to pour out our hearts...

This book enables both carers and those they care for to do just that: through prayer. Here you will find prayers you can adapt to your own situation; also prayers you can join in together. Some prayers look out of the window, and beyond, to remember other sufferers, to lift them into God's presence.

Godfrey Holmes has a remarkable way of putting his finger on so many circumstances, expressing them in the form of prayer to a God who also cares.

I trust this book will be a real blessing for all types of carer and all those needing care. Use it privately. Use it publicly. May you find serenity and strength in your relationship with God and with all those dear to you.

May you truly be "freed for devotion."

Margaret Cundiff

24th May 1999

INTRODUCTION

To picture caring is to picture a bed beside an open French window, flowers, fields and flowing river beyond. Or a high metal bed in some antiseptic hospital ward - flowers a lot nearer, at the bedside, with a few "Get Well Quick" cards. Or else, caring conjures up the image of an upright vinyl-coated ejector seat in some day-room, with television, unwatched, never switched off. Or another, dingier, attic - curtains never drawn back, aspidistra wilting in the corner.

Carers - caring people - summon up equally contrasting images: nurse in starched blue uniform; elderly neighbour - herself rather frail - banging on the next door to check whether "everything's all right"; the unmarried daughter or the middle-aged son back from a day at County Hall; the bright young, enthusiastic, social worker; the willing and extremely loyal teenaged girl, doing all she can before school begins.

A book of prayers specifically for paid and unpaid carers is justified because they face unique challenges and reverses. Caring is a very lonely task, easily forgotten or taken for granted by wider family and the outside world. Caring is also a very introspective task, one that is bound to set the carer thinking about the purpose of being alive, the essence of human relationships, also the nature of a Divinity.

Caring, moreover, is all about healing. That statement seems to refer to the impossible. Surely, caring is about maintaining the existing situation; at best, arresting decline or monitoring decline; at worst, witnessing conditions that have defied all medicines, remedies, or hospital operations.

Carers, nurses, and chaplains increasingly see their role as healing wounded spirits. They are present to give spiritual uplift to those who sometimes despair of merely mechanical interventions. Occasionally, that involves finding more than one person needing encouragement, forgiveness and renewal in a household. In other words, the named sufferer is not always the main sufferer. Jesus alluded to this when he found the Prodigal Son's brother was also lost and when He turned to look at Peter (the Rock) after Peter had denied ever knowing his Master.

Several churches and chapels hold regular healing services. The priests and pastors who conduct these services are rarely "tele-evangelists" who expect, and who stir up, enormous religious fervour: blind people suddenly seeing, paralysed people suddenly walking, much rejoicing in the aisles, weeping and gnashing of teeth.

Healing need not be so dramatic. Better that sufferers and their families are uplifted, and refilled with enthusiasm and hope, than that there be a startling miracle with every laying on of hands.

Mind and body are always inter-linked: majestically, momentously, mysteriously.

Prayers contained within, and suggested by, FREED FOR DEVOTION do attempt to link mind with body, body with mind, mind with an all-seeing God, loving God with loving carer - eventually building bridges between carers in very different settings.

Caring need never be competitive. Distances are great, distractions are many, distinctions few. Why waste energy trying to be better, trying to outdo somebody else, trying to prove a point?

Start the caring day with God, continue the caring day with God; end the caring day with God. "For He cares for you."

HOW TO USE THESE PRAYERS

The carer has five main opportunities for prayer

1) The beginning and end of each day.

    A quiet time demands a certain amount of discipline: the setting aside of a few minutes after waking, and before sleeping. Even ten minutes can leave room for a set prayer, a spontaneous prayer, reading a hymn, a short Bible passage, and perhaps a poem.
    Many prayer books and devotional programmes are set out according to the days of the week or the month.
    These guides and prompts can prove exceptionally useful. They do the choosing for you.
    Parts of FREED FOR DEVOTION can be built into morning or evening quiet times.

2) Church or chapel on a Sunday.

    The reality is that some carers will only be guaranteed specific time to think and to pray during organised worship.
    It is as if a definite Sunday (or weekday) service gives the person praying permission to turn from home, and home responsibilities, to God and God's calling.
    I find it helpful to pray in an empty church building, or in a Cathedral where there are not too many tourists.

3) Dart prayers.

    Dart (or arrow) prayers draw God into the everyday routine, particularly when that routine allows a natural break (eg. bus stop, waiting for the kettle to boil, making the bed, or if the going gets difficult.
    To some extent, dart prayers are not as spontaneous as they first appear. They become a useful habit, similar to the utterances "Hallelujah!" "Hosanna!" "Praise be!" "Yes, Lord!" and "Give me strength!"

4) Specific Occasion Prayers.

    This is where FREED FOR DEVOTION is potentially most useful. Special occasions demand a special response.

Several carers are more nervous on some days than others. I myself find hospital visiting especially difficult. Resuming caring after a break is not easy. Many caring tasks are menial, and exhausting. Additionally, there are times when ageing, suicide or disease are more on our minds than other times. Or when something makes us happier or sadder than usual.

5) Praying With Other People.

Very many people would run a mile, barefoot, rather than pray with other people except when in church or chapel. TV and Radio make praying together unobtrusive, but on other occasions one must surmount the hurdles of embarrassment and reticence.

If an elderly person cares for an elderly partner within the long-term obligation of marriage or partnership - a very common caring arena - then it is natural for the two to pray together, if that has earlier been part of their day or week.

In certain hospitals, hospices, and elderly persons' homes with a Christian foundation, there is nothing exceptional about carer and patient praying together. The same is true where secular establishments employ chaplains of various denominations or none.

Many communities and churches have set up Bereavement Counselling or sick-visitation groups.

In other places, there are helpful House Churches, or midweek prayer-groups. Parts of FREED FOR DEVOTION are written with praying together in mind.

Quite a few carers find prayer letters and printed prayer requests helpful, or asking for a mention on a local or national radio programme. In coming years the Internet will have an important role linking together isolated carers with the outside world: the unlikely successor to CB and CCTV.

Inclusive language is a difficult goal to achieve. In the past I have tried to avoid the term "Lord", for God, because that word has masculine and powerful (or rather, power-based) connotations. I still avoid the term, "Father," for God, first, because many priests are also called Father; second, because many men and women - women in particular - have had negative experiences of father-figures in their lives.

Sometimes, it is impossible not to use "his" or "her" for another person, when praying. In FREED FOR DEVOTION, I sometimes put a gender alternative in brackets, in preference to over-using "their" - which I always consider to be a plural word.

Do add your own set of people's names, or your own terms for the Almighty (another power-based word!)

If you decide to create your own prayers and meditations from scratch, do not hesitate to write down and keep your reflections. Try to stay with one subject only. Don't make your prayers too complicated. God is not more impressed by long words. Do borrow from other people's hymns and prayers.

SECTION 1: UNDERSTANDING

1. **A NEW ROLE IN LIFE**
   O God, in the stillness of this place,
   right early, I call upon Your goodness.
   I hesitate to draw You into the complexity of my situation –
   but I need You now as never before.

   I need You to guide me.   I call upon that guidance.

   I need You to preserve me.   I call upon that preservation.

   I need You to sustain me.   I call upon that sustenance.

   I have probably always been a caring sort of person,
   but I am altering my life to allow caring
   to take greater prominence ...
   That affects my amenability, my availability, my accountability.

   To You I bring my skills.   To You I bring my sympathies.
   To You I bring my suggestions.
   Accept them. Accept me. Use them. Use me.

   And if You cannot stay where I am, show me where You will be,
   and meet me further along the road.

2. **DUTY**
   When I was young,   I ran errands,
                       I washed dishes,
                       I went to Sunday School -
                       out of a sense of Duty.

   Later I gained my school grades
                       and passed my examinations
                       out of a sense of Duty.

   > > >

I rattled collection tins,
> donated my used clothing,
> and picked up litter -
> out of a sense of Duty.

Later still, I applied for jobs,
for extra responsibility,
and for promotion,
again out of a sense of Duty.

Now I am a Carer, I seek to look after another person -
> out of that same sense of Duty.

May Duty never become burdensome and loathsome.
Let me never glory in martyrdom -
> nor ask others to recognise my sacrifice.
And keep me serene fulfilling my Duty, until the day's end.

---

3. SICKNESS

O God, I do not understand sickness
but I do understand wellness and wholeness.
I am so often tempted to say:
> IF ONLY there was no illness;
> IF ONLY there was no suffering;
> IF ONLY there were no viruses and epidemics,
>   no accidents, no broken bones -
>   no infections nor any inflammation;
> IF ONLY there were no hospital operations;
> IF ONLY our bodies did not wear out.

I want a world so well-ordered
that pain and discomfort would disappear.
Yet that cannot be.
So, help me God to understand sickness enough to seek cures;
and to understand the limitations of cures enough to seek the
prevention of all unnecessary sickness.
I ask this through Him who stretched out his hand
to ordinary people who were so unwell.

4. DISABILITY

God, help me not to approach, nor to meet, people with a disability as if they were somehow UNable, or ineligible - as if they were disqualified from wider society.
Let me not address the disability and forget the living person.
Let me not so concentrate on the incapacity as to forget somebody's capacity to think and speak and act.
Let me not build up dependency without considering INdependence.

Save me from categorising the people I meet.
Save me from talking down to them, or above their heads.
Save me from all condescension.

Above all, help me to share MY mobility, MY pride, MY dignity, MY ingenuity, and MY determination
with all those whose mobility, pride, dignity,
ingenuity, and determination would otherwise disappear.

5. OLD AGE

O God,
>   When I was young I could not understand old age -
>   And in older age, I forget my youth.

All things mature
>   trees and plants, coasts and landscapes,
>   games, wines, constitutions, institutions.

People all around me mature.
>   Babies grow into toddlers;
>   Dependent infants grow into self-reliant school children;
>   Gangling teenagers grow into demure young adults;
>   Starry-eyed brides and grooms grow into staid married couples;
>   Newly retired individuals grow into senior citizens.

Help me always to marvel in that growing up,
to assist that growing into; and to rejoice in that growing beyond.
So slow our lives down to a steadier pace.
Make each day more peaceful - and me, more perfect -
till comes the time when all these wheels shall slow down,
and halting, I shall rejoice in the prospect of life everlasting.

6. MENTAL HEALTH

When Jesus encountered evil spirits, those evil spirits fled;
When Jesus encountered a man beside himself with rage,
> that rage subsided;
When Jesus encountered tormented souls,
> He brought peace and hope.

When I am downcast, lift me up;
When I am depressed, pierce the gloom that would envelop me;
When I am beside myself, give me a right mind.

Amidst the clamour of many voices,
> may I distinguish Your still small voice of calm;
In the restlessness of many a sleepless night,
> may I re-discover restfulness;
In disorientation, give me a sense of direction
And in confusion, clarity.

So, as I journey into my inner self,
I shall also find other lost souls along the road.

7. THE NATIONAL HEALTH SERVICE

Lord, I believe in health.
Lord, I believe in a Health Service.

Lord, I pray for health.
Lord, I pray for the National Health Service.

I pray that good health will be available to more people -
and more health available to the few who do not enjoy good health:
because they have no wealth; or those who waste many years in discomfort,
where comfort might only take a few pounds or a few hours to bestow.

May we constantly invest:
not only in our own health, but that of our fellow citizens.
May our privilege extend to those who hitherto have been underprivileged,
and our resourcefulness extend to those who hitherto
have been without resources. To Your Glory.

8. VICTIMS OR SURVIVORS?

When I saw a tramp,
>Jesus saw a traveller;

When I saw an outcast,
>Jesus saw an entrant into the Kingdom of Heaven;

When I saw a leper,
>Jesus saw someone cleansed of every spot;

And when I saw but a corpse,
>Jesus saw someone sound asleep.

Jesus would say: "Take up your bed - and walk!"
Jesus would say: "Go into the Temple;
>declare yourself healed."

And still Jesus is telling us:
>You have before you not a victim - but a survivor;
>someone who is passing from darkness into light;
>someone who is passing from bondage into freedom;
>someone who was last, but is now <u>first</u>.

The very stone the builders rejected has become the head of the corner.
>PRAISE THE LORD!

9. SUICIDE AND ATTEMPTED SUICIDE

Lord, in my imagination, I enter a solitary room:
a cheerless bedsit, a friendless hotel bedroom,
a charmless college study, the cell of a disgraced prisoner.

In my imagination, I climb the bleak cement stairway
to the top of a very high building;
I walk to the cliff-top - not in hope, but in despair
I visit the pharmacist - not to make me well, but ill.
Following such hesitant footsteps,
I try to understand why someone would attempt to take
their own life....

> > >

But I do not understand -
I do not understand such tragic waste of life and health.
I read, but do not understand, those notes that are left behind.
I do not understand that strange mixture
of bravery and cowardice, self-denial and selfishness.
I do not understand the seeming negligence
of parents, brothers, sisters, friends, doctors,
psychiatrists, employers, employees, and persecutors
who might unwittingly have caused such unresolved misery.

Yet let me be slow to condemn -
and quick to join all those who would mend fences,
heal wounds, accept the unaccepted,
and lift those who fall. Who fall as much
in their own estimation as anyone else's.

Lord, let there be fullness of life -
where once there loomed the emptiness of death.

---

10. CARING - PAID OR UNPAID?

Lord, I do not understand
why they are paid to care - when I am unpaid.

They work thirty-seven hours; I work all hours.
They visit many families whereas I have just one family,
in a family home that is sometimes so lonely.

When they are paid,
their ideas are heard and respected and acted on.
My ideas do not count, even if they are listened to.
Paid carers have so much to look forward to:
new jobs, promotion, generous pensions ....
whereas I have nothing to look forward to. I feel so insecure.
I want to rebel; I want to resign.
But nobody would notice my rebellion, or accept my resignation.

Lord, reduce my envy. Lord, increase my commitment.

SECTION 2: SCURRYING

11. TOO BUSY TO THINK
O God,

I asked you for time to think
>to think about happy events in the past,
>what is happening in my life just now
>and to think about the future.

I need time to think -
>yet I am too busy to think.

Every day I am plunged straight into the work
>of looking after (another/others)

And when I have finished,
>it is time to start all over again.

Yes: I do need that time to think
>or else I shall lose my bearings.

I ask You for time to think.

12. MANY BUCKETS AND BOWLS
Amidst the cluster of buckets
>and the clanking of bowls;

Amidst the draining of sinks
>and the flushing of cisterns;

Amidst the mopping of floors
>and the sponging of bibs;

Amidst the disposal of used linen
>and the tumbling of fresh towels;

Amidst all those caring activities
>least glamorous, most unproductive:

Give us remembrance of Jesus
>who knelt to wash the dusty feet of his longsuffering disciples,
>that same Jesus whose seamless robe
>was dragged through the dirt and spattered with blood.

13. MANY ERRANDS
Upstairs. Downstairs.
Downstairs. Upstairs.
To the chemist. Back from the chemist.
To the surgery. On to the hospital.
Calling the specially adapted coach.
Boarding the specially adapted coach.
To benefits office. Back via Social Services.

Many errands of mercy
Hither and thither,
Whither and whether

Often would I stay in bed where it's warm.
Often would I stay indoors where it's cosy.
Often would I say NO - where You say Go!

14. MANY PEOPLE TO CONSULT
They said I was part of a caring team
the doctor, the nurse, the physiotherapist, the occupational therapist,
the counsellor, the auxiliary and the social worker.

For a while I was happy to be a team member until that team
closed ranks and left me outside; until that team moved on,
and left me behind.

Soon it was a team obeying orders that were not my orders.
Soon it was a team thinking ideas that were not my ideas.

There are still so many people I should want to consult
or to be consulted by.
In many ways, Lord, I yearn for privacy.
I yearn to manage on my own as best I can.
In time,
make me less resentful of all this external interference;
and make me more committed to progress which is only possible
because others would want to interfere.

15. TRYING TO RUN A HOUSEHOLD
O God, I cannot run this household properly
    because of my caring responsibility.

Clothes washing piles up;
I am behind with the ironing;
I have not even thought about baking.

I know that most carers have houses to run as well.
Yet they can often leave their homes behind
when they go out to work ...

Whereas, I stop indoors to work.

That is when I notice not what I've done,
but what I've left undone.
Even when I'm away a short while,
I dread coming back to find out all I should be doing.

O God, give me the will to do everything which can be done,
and the detachment to leave everything which can't be done.

16. WORKING LATE TONIGHT
I'm working late tonight -
Just as I was working late last night.

I shall probably be working late tomorrow night also.

There were days I'd look forward to the night-time;
    the drawing in of the day, the drawing to of the curtains,
    withdrawing to watch television,
        to converse, to play games, or to rest.

I know deep down: I should not work nights
when I have worked right through the day;
or day, when I have worked through the night.

Lord of day and night -
Lord of engagement and disengagement:
Grant me now the repose that is my due.

17. BRINGING UP CHILDREN AS WELL

One child cries
I hear (her) not.
One child opens (her) mouth to speak;
I'm not inclined to listen.

The child who looks to me for comfort
    goes away uncomforted.
The child who looks to me for confidence
    goes away betrayed.
And the child who looks to me for advice
    goes away clueless.

I neglect the well child in order to care for the ill child
Or else I neglect the ill child to care for the iller parent,
the iller grand-parent, the iller aunt or uncle, or the iller neighbour.

I find I have love, but may not show it;
I have patience and understanding - but may not show that either.
Divide me up, Lord, as You see fit.

18. A BABY WITH ONLY A LITTLE TIME TO LIVE

I hold in my arms this little bundle of life -
or else I look through the glass.

I connect all the tubing;
I listen for any alarming noises.

The nurse has told me there's no hope for this baby
The doctor has told me (s)he has so little time to live.

Even as I pray, the undertaker is preparing his carriage.
These are sombre times for me and for the baby's wider family.

All our love and attention must be fitted into so few hours.
As You have granted me attentiveness, may it show;
As You have granted me such love, may it flow.

May the tiny life now fluttering be like a candle
flickering on the stairway to heaven.

19. CARING BEFORE GOING TO SCHOOL
School starts soon
all too soon.

I have many jobs still to do
before school gates swing open
and a bell sounds for start of lessons.
School is what defines each school day,
yet I am unprepared for school -
until I have completed my caring tasks here.

You asked that I should love learning -
yet so much of my learning takes place right here.

You only promised a book
that those who run might read.

20. CARING AFTER A FULL DAY AT WORK
Hello! I'm back, back home.
Another day done
>   all files closed,
>   all products packed,
>   all customers satisfied
>   windows locked, floors cleaned.

There was a time, once,
>   when I could now put my feet up,
>   read the paper,
>   enjoy my dinner,
>   listen to music.

Yet must I turn to my second job,
in a way, my far more demanding job:
Caring for someone who needs me more
than those I've worked for all day -
many of whom I do not know,
and certainly do not love.

Give me now new energy,
new enthusiasm, new endurance.

SECTION 3: SHIELDING

21. NOT MENTIONING MYSELF
O God: I am so concentrating on problems
which are not mine,
and situations that are not of my own making,
and people outside my sphere of influence -
that I make no mention of myself, and my needs.

In conversation with my friends, I make no mention of myself.
At social gatherings, I make no mention of myself.
In Church, I make no mention of myself.
And in correspondence, I hardly make mention of myself.

I have decreased so that the person(s) I care for may increase.

Yet You are still there to recognise, to promote,
and to safeguard my needs -
even those needs I do not know I need.

Let me never be ashamed of myself and my selfhood.
Daily might I mention myself alongside all others.

22. NOT TALKING ABOUT THE ILLNESS
O God, I want to find out so much more
about the suffering of the person(s) I care for.

I want to understand their frailty,
the onset, the progress and the outcome of their disability.
I want to know about all the treatments
scientists and doctors have discovered or attempted.
Yet in my efforts to talk about health, and healthy signs,
I am tempted to overlook ill-health and unhealthy signs.

Give me to know enough to be more useful -
but not so much that I become obsessed with it all.

23. NOT TAKING ALL RESPONSIBILITY FROM OTHER PEOPLE

Many days, Lord, I'm in the foreground: I'm in charge.
That gives me satisfaction and some measure of control.

But no squad can prosper with just one star-player
and there are so many times when I am that star-player.

When I am tempted to make all the right moves,
and - yes - receive all the honours.

Turn my head upwards to You for my strength -
then sideways to all the people in the shadows,
all the people on the sidelines,
who would happily share the task -
if only I would call on them.

24. NOT CHALLENGING WHEN PEOPLE TALK DOWN TO ME

I am the doorpost;
Walk past me.
I am the doorpost;
Speak past me.
I am the doorpost;
Look not at me.
I am the doorpost;
Think not of me.
I am the doorpost;
Make me shudder.
I am the doorpost;
Make me shiver.
I am the doorpost;
still there - when everyone else has gone.
I am the doorpost, Lord.

25. NOT ARGUING WITH THE PERSON(S) I AM CARING FOR
Life is too short
for me, the looker-after,
to shout at the person(s) I am looking after ...

Because their lifespan has been unexpectedly shortened,
their life-chances unexpectedly shaded.
Despite that, some days are far too long and tedious
for the person(s) I am looking after - each day much like the day before.

Sometimes I lose my temper, You know I do.
Sometimes I bicker and hector, You know I do.
Some weeks, I rattle and am too easily rattled.
You, Lord, know everything.

In this caring role, I need to be a proper person with sensible reaction.
Set a guard on my tongue - lest it cause needless hurt or pain.

26. NOT DOING EVERYTHING
Lord , I am so capable ...
I want to do absolutely everything
All the cooking, all the feeding,
All the fetching, all the carrying,
All the writing, all the reading,
All the lifting, all the holding.

I so want to do everything -
that I take on those tasks I hate.
Then I hate myself for being so obliging.

I so want to do everything -
that I let the rest of the family do nothing.
I so want to do everything -
that I scarcely allow the person(s) I care for
to do anything, either -
so taking away all their confidence.

Increase my trust in other people
to share the load so that,
when I appear to do less, I do more.

27. NOT PRESSURISING THE PERSON(S) I CARE FOR

When (s)he is off food,
I want _____ to eat.
When (s)he is off-colour,
I want _____ to spark up.
When (s)he is off-hand,
I want _____ to be more even-tempered.
And when (s)he is obstinate
I want _____ to give way and to get going.

I am tempted to <u>force</u> _____ to give way.
So it is I <u>demand</u> that _____ eats.
So it is I anticipate that _____ sparks up.
So it is I insist that _____ becomes more even-tempered.

Father forgive me for I know not what I do.

28. NOT CORRECTING

Lord, in my caring task
I would seek to correct.

I would correct mistaken sentiments;
I would correct mistaken facts;
I would correct mistaken opinions;
I would correct mistaken judgements -
especially of people we both know.

Most of all, I would correct mistaken memories.

Yet, in time, might I see that it is not always
my responsibility to correct everything.
Sometimes it is my responsibility to correct nothing.

Yes, Lord, I know some people think that is the easiest option.
Other people think, "anything for a quiet life."
Perhaps that quietness, that peace and goodwill,
is usually more important than the original error.

29. NOT FORBIDDING

Forbid it that I should always be forbidding
    on hot days, forbidding hot meals;
    on wet days, forbidding venturing out;
    on Lottery days, forbidding gambling;
    on feast days, forbidding alcohol;

and on all days, forbidding escapist reading,
    forbidding trashy viewing,
    forbidding raucous listening.

I even forbid too much hospitality -
    in case we are lumbered with bores and busybodies.
That used to be my goal, to forbid -
    where sometimes the better way would be to allow.

30. NOT RESIGNING

You know, O God, how often I am tempted to resign
to walk out,
to leave the heat and the kitchen,
to put a note under the teapot,
to put everything and everyone behind me...

Tolerating no more, attempting no more, persevering no more.

Yet it is far harder to stay.
That is what Jesus discovered in the carpenter's shop;
or later by the Sea of Galilee when crowds hemmed Him in;
as visitor within a private home, when onlookers gawped at Him;
finally in Jerusalem, visible, a sitting target for arrest -
when he could have been far away, invisible - and safe.

If I do this day decide to stay, may I stay gladly.
And may I never use the temptation to go as a threat.

SECTION 4: ADVISING

31. GIVE ME THE RIGHT ADVICE TO PASS ON
Lord, there are few responsibilities
more awesome than passing on the right advice:

that "word in season" as from You.

Let some of my advice be as the Spring:
    fresh and sprouting.
Let some of my advice be as the Summer:
    warm and plentiful.
Let some of my advice be as the Autumn:
    mature and wholesome;
and let some of my advice be as the Winter:
    stark and unrelenting.

Make me neither proud nor precious about the advice I dispense,
and never downcast when that advice is ignored or rejected.

This I ask in Your Name, and for Your sake.

32. GIVE ME ALL KNOWLEDGE ABOUT BENEFITS
I don't know who decided to call money a "benefit."
I don't even know whether everyone who receives
state money benefits from it.
Or whether claimants benefit fully.
Or how much claimants would need to receive
in order to benefit fully.
How shall I know when claimants have benefited enough?

All these benefits are so confusing.
Sometimes we claim too little.
Other times we claim too much.
Sometimes we claim too eagerly.
Other times we claim far too hesitantly.

How easily we forgo those benefits we are entitled to.
All I now need to grasp is what money is available,
when and where - especially for carers like me
and the people we care for.
Where St. Peter and St. Paul did not hesitate to seek
the sustenance that was their due, let me not hesitate either.

33. HELP ME TO NEGOTIATE

O God my task of caring also involves negotiation:
for more help, more money, more control, more consultation.

I do have limits on my goodwill.
And those with whom I negotiate also have their limits.
People I do not see - but who write, or telephone,
or hold influence behind the scenes have their limits too.

Negotiating is very difficult.
None of us is entirely sure of the strength of our position.
And we all hate to lose face, or to lose ground.

In all my negotiations, make me firm, yet persistent.

Weigh me not down with the knowledge
that someone else will lose out if I or the one(s) I care for win -
though keep that ever in the back of my mind.
And, let me never seek to win at all costs, for that is too expensive.

34. DIRECTING SOMEONE SOMEWHERE ELSE

You know how sometimes I am so keen
to direct somebody somewhere else.
Caring is such an enormous task that often
"somewhere else" appears a safer, speedier,
and more successful option.

Yet when I do direct someone somewhere else,
help me to scale down their high expectations ...
because they will have had those expectations dashed
on other occasions without number.

May I never wish that my friend or enquirer
simply goes away.
I ask this in the name of Jesus
who empowered so many of his disciples
to carry on exactly where He had to leave off.

35. SEEING MY ADVICE IGNORED
O God, I see my advice being ignored.
Worse, I see my advice not listened to in the first place.

At these moments, I am tempted to offer no more advice to anyone -
nor to accept any more advice from anyone.

I can never understand why some people are so stubborn,
so short-sighted, so suspicious.

Perhaps to follow my advice would involve change
or at least a change of direction, and the person(s)
seeking my advice might fear change above all else.

Still give me respect for all those who ask me what to do.
Make me content in the knowledge that it takes many seeds
sown for a few plants to flourish.

36. SEEING MY ADVICE OVERRULED
Sometimes, O Lord, I see my advice overruled.
I suggest what is feasible.
    It is dismissed as impossible.
I suggest what is affordable.
    It is dismissed as extravagant.
I suggest what is worthwhile.
    It is dismissed as of little value.
And I suggest what is achievable.
    It is relegated to bottom of the pile.

Prevent my disheartenment.
Prevent my indignation.
Always.

37. PUSHING

I see a door ahead of me - marked PUSH.
And I think of all life's pushers:
>Those who push trolleys in the supermarket;
>Those who push stretcher-beds in hospital;
>Those who push wheelchairs over uneven pavements;
>Those who push bins full of rubbish;
>Those who push little children to playgroup;
>Those who push older children to pass their exams;
>Those who push ideas and inventions;
>Those who push products, books and films;
>and
>Those who push their side of each story.

Pushing is an interesting and influential task -
especially when the pusher sees the result of all the pushing.

Save me from becoming obsessed with my cause
when it is I who does the pushing.

38. PULLING

I see a door ahead of me saying: PULL
and I think of all those people who spend their hours
and their days pulling:

Pulling	heavy loads,
Pulling	strings
Pulling	ropes,
Pulling	chains,
Pulling	ships,
Pulling	people out of wreckage,
	out of danger,
	or out of their beds.

It strikes me that pullers are even busier than pushers,
and that pulling requires even more effort than pushing.

When I need to pull, give me that extra strength -
also the foresight not to make matters far worse
than they were when first I accepted the challenge.

39. TIRED OF THE TELEPHONE

The telephone stopped ringing - and I gazed at the dial.

1. was one lonely person who would call me next;
2. were the two twisted souls who would call threateningly: breathing heavily, breathing hatred;
3. were the three time wasters who would call as a hoax, hoping to shock;
4. were the four people who would find the line engaged and go elsewhere;
5. were the five tormented people so wanting to call, but without courage enough to lift the receiver;
6. were the six target groups for telephone help-lines: those suicidal, disabled, confused; those overburdened, bereaved, or accused;
7. were just seven of seventy times seven premium-rate call lines and chat lines;
8. were eight reasons given for sudden repression: "I was aggravated - provoked - drunk – tired misled - mismatched - misquoted – misunderstood;"
9. were the nine lives of the proverbial cat... against all the odds - surviving and thriving.

Then I looked at Nought: Nought for their Comfort?
I hope not. Nought to regret when I put down that receiver...
that is what I should want.

This strange, but wonderful, instrument
help me to use to Your glory.

40. TIRED OF GIVING OUT ADVICE

Lord, I don't want to give out any more advice:
not to anyone, on any count.
My advice is too precious to be wasted.

People come along with very difficult problems, problems far too difficult to solve .... Yet they want a solution straightaway:
in such a way that I am left holding the problem, working and worrying on someone else's behalf where the persons who used to own that problem walk free. Carefree. >>>

There are now so many other sources of advice,
    so many agencies, and magazine columns,
    and telephone helplines.
Yet, today, there might be <u>one</u> person lost to self,
lost to family, and lost to society.

In that case, I shall matter and my advice will matter:
"Some act of love begun, Some deed of kindness done,
Some wanderer sought and won : Something for Thee."

SECTION 5: BEFRIENDING

41. THE PRISONER
O God,
Whose Son Jesus is the Guardian of all those who are imprisoned.

Jesus Christ,	Hope of all those who are imprisoned;
Jesus Christ,	Inspiration of all prisoners guilty of no offence;
Jesus Christ,	Forgiver of all prisoners guilty of terrible offences;
Jesus Christ,	Forerunner of St. Paul of Tarsus,
	Successor of John the Baptist - prisoners both;
Jesus Christ,	Yourself held captive in a dark cell;
Jesus Christ,	whose truth does set us free:

Give me a way into prison,
and a way into the hearts of prisoners;
And give prisoners a way out of prison -
out of the confines of greed and malice and revenge.
And help us all – imprisoned or liberated –
to tear down the barbed fences of dishonesty, hatred and violence.

42. THE DRUNKARD
Lord, I see alcohol everywhere:
> in street, in supermarket, in hotel,
> behind every bar, on many a sideboard.

And I am overawed by the power of strong drink to affect,
to change, and to destroy not only other people's lives,
but my own life.

I remember the drunkard I saw at the railway station.
I remember the drunkard I saw in the cemetery.
I remember the drunkard I saw at the party.
I remember the drunkard I saw behind the wheel of a car.
And I remember the drunkard I saw sprawled out on the pavement.

> > >

I was tempted to say: "That's only a drunkard,"
until I stopped to think here is someone
who could have followed in Your pathways had he not strayed.

In my drinking, make me temperate;
In the example I set, make me vigilant;
And in my befriending of those who have drunk too much,
make me cautious, understanding, and forgiving.

---

43. HOMELESS PEOPLE

I gave them a cornerstone that their building would not shudder;
I gave them some bricks that they should have walls;
I gave them a floor that they might sleep on it;
I gave them a roof that beneath it they might shelter from the elements;
I gave them a window also - that they might look out of it.

And when the last cart left, I said: "Here is your home."
And I told them that to have any home is so much better
than to have no home.
But still they said, "This is not our home."

Vainly I offered them a bench, a tub, a fire-place - yet still they said,
"This is not our home."

So it was that I remembered love, a love stronger
than mere liking, a commitment firmer than mere promise.
I entered their building with love.
"Now," they said, "this is our home."

44. WIDOWS AND WIDOWERS

Lord, I see a streak of lightning: it cuts a tree in two.
I see the blade of a very sharp knife: it cuts a loaf in two.
I see a mighty highway: it cuts a town in two.
I see a high fence of barbed wire, to cut a field in two.
So it is that death makes widows of women, and widowers of men.

Their lives are cut in two.
From now on, they are lonely individuals:
cell-mates instead of the soul-mates they were.

In my ministry to people left behind by tragedy foreseen
and by tragedies unforeseen,
give me inspiration and enlightenment;
also the sensitivity not to expect reaction, explanation, consolation
from those who cannot muster reaction, nor offer explanation,
nor derive consolation.

45. TEENAGERS

O God, it is often so difficult to befriend teenagers:
They always appear to be just a bit beyond reach.
Maybe they have private thoughts, and a thirst for privacy;
Maybe they have a language, a fashion, a rhythm
or an interest that I do not appreciate;
Maybe they are shy and I am shy;
Maybe they are nervous and I am nervous;
Maybe they are around when I am not around;
or they are flippant when I am serious -
or they are careless when I try to be so careful.

Perhaps as I search teenagers out, they are still a way ahead.

Help me not to give up at the first hurdle, the first insult,
the first rejection, or the first impossible demand.

Instead, help me to be as I am, to enjoy being who I am:
joking, jostling, jousting, juggling... just like them.

46. FAMILIES AT RISK

Lord, there are so many families at risk: thousands of families in this country, millions of families overseas -
- At risk of destitution,
- At risk of under-nourishment,
- At risk of disease,
- At risk of warfare,
- At risk of violence, within, without,
- At risk of harmful substances,
- At risk of the depletion of natural resources,

Families at risk of being broken up,
and families at risk of never becoming established in the first place.
Sometimes I shall not know exactly how much risk families do face.
Instead, I shall have to guess the risk, or assume the risk,
or let the risk increase before it can decrease.
Some days families most at risk will flee, or hide,
or split before I get there.
Other days, I shall conclude it is not a question of families at risk,
but the very institution of the family at risk, given so little backing
- morally,
- spiritually,
- practically,
- or financially.

I feel tempted to give up in despair ...
to let families deteriorate
because any alternative would be too hard to negotiate.

Perhaps if I befriended just one family;
Perhaps if I remembered in my prayers another family;
Perhaps if I told somebody else about a third family at risk;
Then some of those hitherto without hope might gain,
whilst other families hitherto without gain
would have somewhere to attach their hope.

47. WOMEN ENDURING DOMESTIC VIOLENCE
Lord help me in my feeling for,
    my interceding for,
    my labouring for,
women enduring domestic violence.
Silent or vocal they, make my support unwavering;
Departing or returning they, make my support unwavering;
Sinking or swimming they, make my support unwavering;
"Deserving" or innocent they, make my support unwavering;
Loyal or disloyal they, make my support unwavering.

Help me never to impose my choices, my judgements, my solutions upon these women so uncertain about their futures.
Help me simply to be around, and attentive when needed, and to disappear when not needed.
And may I never give comfort, excuse, or tacit approval to any emotional or mental or physical or sexual cruelty within the home - nor solace to anybody who perpetrates, or perpetuates, such cruelty.

48. PARENTS WHO MISTREAT THEIR CHILDREN
Sometimes, God, parents and step-parents are very forgetful or neglectful towards their children and their partners' children.
    I remember before You children who are unfed and unwashed.
    I remember before You children who are unheeded and unloved.
    I remember before You children who are locked in or locked out, those who are always in the wrong or who are never told what is right.

Also I would remember before You those many children who only ever see their parent-figures depressed and oppressed.
I know that sometimes I shall be called upon to befriend some parents who have acted harshly; others who have not stepped in to prevent harshness when they have seen it, or heard it.

Let me never condemn parents whose hearts are set
on doing the best they know how.
Even then, let me show them new patterns of parenting,
more generous parenting, more responsible parenting - to Your glory.

49. THOSE WHO INFLICT SELF-HARM

Lord, I need to befriend people who have inflicted self-harm,
those who - rather than he further abused - abuse themselves,
those who - rather than suffer in silence - suffer under the glare of
hospital lamps.

I confess I do not always comprehend self-harm, nor the reasons
behind self-harm: miseries, tensions, pressures concealed, potential
unfulfilled, goals unattained.
I do not always comprehend that urgent need to be noticed and valued,
nor the sudden relief and release that accompanies self-harm.
What a waste of health, a waste of life: self-harm indicating concern,
not unconcern; acquisition, not abandonment.

Where there is overdose, let there be detoxification;
Where there is wounding, let there be anointment;
Where a mind has become distracted, let there be composure;
And where self-neglect and mutilation has already hastened death,
still let there be freedom from torment or recrimination.

50. COMPLETE STRANGERS

People I lived with found me there.
People I worked with found me there.
People I mixed with found me there.
People I relaxed with found me there.

It was easy to be a friend to those who befriended me;
to be a neighbour to those who were my neighbours;
and to be aware of the troubles of those
whose very existence I was closely aware of.

Forgive me: I was not always so alert to the complete stranger.
When a stranger called me, I did not always hear.
When a stranger required something of me,
I did not always respond.

You know how difficult it is to talk to a complete stranger,
how difficult it is to interfere when interference is resented;
to help, when that act of helping is misguided, misunderstood.
Still make me, Lord, the first to hold out my hand,
and the last to take it back; the first to leap, the last to stay put.

SECTION 6: SHARING

51. I WANT TO DONATE MORE TO CHARITY
I want to give more to charity and to good causes,
if only I can set aside the right amount of money -
and send it to the right place.
Sometimes I am so confused about all the charities I hear about:
those that rattle their tins, those that send me their literature.

I am always muddled by their aims and objectives.
I am always uncertain how much they spend on self-promotion
and self-preservation, how much on needy people and animals.
I am bewildered by sponsorship, raffles, stunts, bazaars,
banquets and bequests.

Lord, let me never use my perplexity as excuse not to give
anything at all, anywhere, anytime.
Let all my small donations become great offerings in Your sight;
until my left hand really does not know what my right hand does;
until my compassion shines far brighter
than the coin I took from my pocket.

52. I WANT TO GIVE SOMETHING ELSE
I am perplexed.
If I give money to charity, I meet collectors not recipients;
If I collect money for charity, I meet donors not recipients;
And if I ask for money to be taken direct from, my salary,
or my bank account, for some good cause,
I meet neither collectors nor other donors, still less recipients.
I did think of offering my services to a good cause -
perhaps working in their charity shop, perhaps in their office -
but still I fear I would not meet recipients.

Who is keeping me away?

Give me courage to cross that great divide - without condescension
or self-congratulation; without intruding into grief,
without patronising those I meet, or smothering them, or bossing them.
Without gawping at them, or photographing them.
And once over that divide, give me the conviction to remain
there however long I am still needed.

53. I'M THINKING OF OPENING MY HOME
TO AGEING PARENT(S)

Lord, I don't know whether to go ahead and open this home of mine
to my ageing parent(s)
[to my partner's ageing parent(s)].
Part of me thinks I should respond to their growing incapacity,
[disorientation] by extending my household.
Part of me feels it my duty to provide
a dignified end to a life [lives] well-lived.

Part of me wants to open my heart as well as my home.

But part of me is fearful, perplexed, even depressed.
Part of me wonders if I am biting off more than I can chew.
Part of me would rather give up now:
closing the door straightway, before it is open but a crack.
Help me, O God, whatever my eventual decision,
to act conscientiously and humanely - above all, appropriately.

54. I WANT TO SHARE MY SPARE TIME

I have lived for myself
immersed in my own interests
far too long.

I should like now to share more of my spare time with
    Somebody disabled,
    Somebody needy,
    Somebody confused,
    Somebody elderly,
    Somebody ill, or
    Somebody underfunctioning.

Show me how to do this,
just when and where.
Above all, show me how to start,
independently or in concert with others.
And let me never be distracted by those who would
criticise both my motivation and my level of skill.

55. I WANT TO FOSTER
Lord, I want to foster,
to open my house and heart to many children:
Children in need - children abused, neglected,
rejected; children born too early or too late;
children angry, ungrateful, spiteful;
children who have had no proper childhood,
no proper schooling, no proper handling;
children who have rarely been praised
       for any aspects of their personalities,
       for any talents or accomplishments,
       for any acts of generosity or self-denial,
       for anything they are wearing,
       or studying, or collecting.

Yes Lord, I want to foster.
I pray that You will oversee my application,
and all the deliberations of those
who will deal with my application.
And, even now, Lord, begin to enter the lives
of those young people who will one day come my way.

56. I WANT TO ADOPT
Lord, I want to adopt.

At first, that desire appears to be crazy.
There are so few babies up for adoption.

There are so few problem-free toddlers suitable for adoption.
There are so few undamaged younger children released for adoption.
And there are so few teenagers expressing the wish to be adopted.
As if that were not discouragement enough,
if I were to adopt the child of a relation or friend,
or even a terribly disadvantaged child from overseas,
all sorts of obstacles would be placed in my way.
If still I should want to adopt, may I proceed confidently and
unashamedly ready for any disappointment,
any intrusiveness, any reversal, any outcome.

57. I WANT TO MARRY SOMEONE WITH A DISABILITY

I feel half incomplete.
The real me is to spare.
The real me is there to share.

I now want to marry someone with a disability.

I enter this circumspectly;
I enter this intelligently;
I enter this spiritually;
Yes, Lord, I enter this self-sacrificially....

but knowing I shall gain far more than I shall ever lose.

Remove from my life any deceit, any self-indulgence.

Free me from people who might praise me,
or pity me, or pester me.
Let me always think before I respond to the struggles ahead.
Then let my response be guided always by my beliefs
and Your unfailing belief in me.

58. I WANT TO SHARE CARING WITH THE REST OF MY FAMILY

Lord, I cannot continue alone;

I dare not continue on my own;

I should not continue on my own;

I must not continue on my own.

I can now ask the rest of my family;

I dare now ask the rest of my family;

I should now ask the rest of my family;

I must now ask the rest of my family.

You gave us families for support.

Lead this family to come to support me, as I pray.

59. MY FAITH
Lord, I am shy
shy to discuss my faith with the person(s) I am caring for.

They might have different beliefs from mine - or none;

Or else their beliefs might have been dented, diminished or even deadened by the pain and suffering they have endured;

Or else they might feel that here they are a captive audience;
that they are unable to argue, or to protest, or to switch off - because they depend on me.
Yet let me boldly proclaim with my lips - importantly, with my life - where I come from, and where my faith leads me.

In the name of Jesus who spread his message far and wide.

60. I WANT TO SHARE MY OPTIMISM
O Eternal One:
In my dreams I climb a mountain.
But every few yards, my feet slip on the shale.
I climb higher.
But there is a wide ravine ahead.
I slide, uncontrolled, until
I clutch a tree.
Higher still, I cross a bog.
In no time, I am up to my knees in slush, mud and slime.
Then I see the summit.
But in between is a glacier, glistening in clear, sharp, sunshine.
Still I persevere, until that moment when I stand higher than all the world below me.
So assist me as I climb life's daily mountains that somehow I might discover optimism, maintain optimism, eventually: share optimism.
To Your Glory.

SECTION 7: VISITING

61. HOSPITAL
Lord, I am visiting hospital today.
At the main entrance I shall find:
> nervous people, disorganised people,
> bewildered people, overburdened people.

Then, in Accident and Emergency I shall find:
> crushed people, shocked people,
> broken people, hysterical people.

On the wards I shall find:
> patients operated upon, patients awaiting operation,
> patients recovering, patients deteriorating.

And in the corridors I shall find:
> some visitors waiting, other visitors crying,
> some visitors appreciative, other visitors apprehensive

Throughout the hospital today, I shall find:
diligent staff, distracted staff, staff overwhelmed, staff undervalued.
Lord, whoever I meet: by chance or on purpose,
my responsibility or someone else's, living or dying –
Supply me with: words of kindness, words of compassion,
words of comfort, words of encouragement;
And: the silence of concord, the silence of sharing, the silence of tact,
the silence of petition.

62. A SPECIAL SCHOOL
Today I am visiting a special school - a school
only for children with some extra need
only for children wanting extra guidance and supervision,
only for children who could not survive the extra pressures
of life in a mainstream school.

These Your children have special gifts,
and a special way of exploring regions I take for granted.
These Your children have capacities of which I am incapable,
insights into which I have no sight;
experiences way beyond my experience. > > >

If it sometimes disturbs the outsider to meet an unusual child,
how daunting it is to meet a dozen, a hundred,
all in one place at one time.
Make my visit go well today.

Save me from grinning. Save me from staring.
And save me from looking so uncomfortable
that I make staff and scholars alike
feel uncomfortable in my presence.

---

63. A HOSTEL
Today I am visiting a hostel:

odd, because all the residents have a choice about being there –
yet few actively chose to go there in the first place.

I shall not enter a bedroom unless its resident invites me in.
Bedrooms are private spaces.
Those who intrude, even to do good, or to seek good,
invade a very special space.

Perhaps, God, this is how You intended men and women to live
in hostels as communities: each person depending on all.

Bless this community I shall be entering.
Bless each friendship forged, each venture attempted,
each decision reached, each disagreement settled.

So grant this community I shall be visiting security and vitality.

64. A HOSPICE
Lord, I am not looking forward to this my visit to a hospice.

> I do not know that I am prepared enough.
> I do not know what I shall see.
> I do not know what I shall hear.
> I do not know what I shall think.
> Worst of all, I do not know what I shall say.

When I arrive, should I concentrate on death or on life?

What I do know is that all those patients
I shall meet need love and attention, feeding and cleansing.

To You I commit my journey.
To You I commit their journey.
To You I commit the staff of this hospice:
employees and volunteers alike in their comings and goings,
their ministry, their own mortality.

65. A CHILDREN'S HOME
I have mixed feelings about visiting a children's home.
Some of these establishments appear to do more harm than good:
leading vulnerable teenagers into greater personal risk,
greater chance of offending.
I know some of the staff I meet will be dedicated
others will be there on sufferance,
their vocation tested to an extreme.

Bless, I pray, all children whose days in Care
become months and years;
all children who are orphaned, abandoned, addicted,
assaulted, rejected;
all who have a temperament or a disability
which their parents cannot manage;
or whose parents cannot manage each other's,
or society's demands.

Save all children and staff within children's homes
from feeling isolated, marginalised or undervalued.
So, might this forgotten building radiate again
light and warmth and hope.

66. SOMEONE WHO IS DEPRESSED

Today (tomorrow) I shall visit someone who is very depressed.
I might get no answer at all when I knock on the door.
Or I might not gain entry even when the door is opened.
Or I might get inside only to find myself talking empty pleasantries.
Or else I shall wallow in the same sea of depression
as the person I am worried about,
or float down my own river of despair towards that sea.
In other words, My God, I am frightened to go.
I should rather go to see somebody a little more cheerful -
who can help <u>me</u> a little more.
I understand less about depression than the person who is depressed.
You have sent me once. Perhaps You will send me many times.
Now I see through a glass darkly; then, face-to-face.

67. SOMEONE WHO HAS HAD AN ACCIDENT

To-day (tomorrow) I shall visit someone who has had an accident.
Why? Oh Why? (s)he rages.
Why? Oh Why? I rage.
I could accept an infection or a known bodily illness.

I could even accept a psychiatric illness.

But this accident was so pointless.
In retrospect, it was so avoidable.

I rage at the negligence, the recklessness, that allowed it to happen:
the utter waste of life or limb.

Still help me to go with an open heart and mind,
ready to make my visit soothing, warming, and uplifting.
May I let time and due processes do their own inquiring.
But, when I am leaving the injured one, make my own driving,
moving, handling, and holding,
ever more cautious, ever safer.

68. SOMEONE BEREAVED
Today (tomorrow) I must visit someone recently bereaved.

Fill me with overflowing sympathy: a shared grief.

Save me from avoiding talking about loss;
Save me from minimising that loss;
Save me equally from exaggerating that loss;
Save me from anticipating future compensation(s);
And save me from assuming that her (his)
loss is the same as the loss I faced when a loved one died.
Save me most of all, O God, from a pride in people
and possessions I have retained at a time
when this other person has been so hugely robbed.
And make me daily prepared to live or die to Your wondrous glory.

69. SOMEONE WHO HAS BEEN BURGLED
Today (tomorrow) I shall be visiting someone who has been burgled:
someone who has come in, come back, come down,
or come round to find treasures missing, belongings damaged,
drawers upturned, doors unhinged, familiar territories invaded.

Give me the right words of comfort;
Give me the right spirit of generosity;
Give me the right level of anger and indignation.

I do not know really what to expect -
because the whole dire situation is so unexpected.
Maybe I am going in order to do as beckoned.

Ever make me glad that the sanctuary of my heart
cannot be burgled or defiled while ever You dwell therein.
Ever make me glad that nobody can take way the gift
of Your Son who went round doing good,
who taught in parables, who performed many miracles,
who was crucified, yet rose again.

70. SOMEONE WHO HAS RECENTLY RELINQUISHED CARING

Today (tomorrow) I shall be visiting someone who has recently given up the task of caring for some other person(s).

At first this devoted carer will feel bewildered.
At first this devoted carer will feel disorientated.
At first this devoted carer will feel redundant.
And, certainly, unrecognised.

Worse will be the impact if (s)he sees somebody else
take over the caring task, as if to do it more efficiently.
Or if (s)he sees somebody else doing the same caring task,
but for a different person (set of people).

Then will come the time when the ex-carer I visit will try
and even fail to carve out a new niche at home,
or school, or work, or church, or neighbourhood.
There will be many tears, many trials, many torments -
many memories I shall need to share.
Give me new strength and insight in my mission.

SECTION 8: PRAYING TOGETHER

71. A PRAYER FOR HEALING
Lord God, I pray for Your healing touch.

Lord Jesus, I pray for Your healing touch;
> the touch that cured the ten lepers;
> the touch that raised Jairus' daughter;
> the touch that gave back sight to a blind beggar;
> the touch that restored a withered arm;
> the touch that raised Lazarus from the dead;
> the touch that stopped one woman's bleeding;
> the touch that rid one man of a host of evil spirits;
> the touch that allowed another man to put away his stretcher;
> the touch that healed a soldier's ear;
> the touch that filled multitudes of people with envy
> and hope, wonder and thanksgiving.

I know that healing touch is still there,
for all who live by faith and believe in Your saving presence:
Today and always.

72. HELPING EACH OTHER
At the start of each day
In our rising, our washing, our dressing -
Your strength is sufficient for us.

At the noon of each day:
In our catering, our exercising, our shopping -
Your strength is sufficient for us.

At the dusk of each day:
In our letter-writing, our phoning, our visiting -
Your strength is sufficient for us.

At the close of each day:
In our planning, our praying, our lying down to rest -
Your strength is sufficient for us. > > >

And through the long night:
In our agonising, our watching, our waiting -
Your strength is sufficient for us.

At each stage of our lives:
Your strength is sufficient for us.

---

73. SEEING A GOAL

O God who commanded us through Your holy apostle
to run the race boldly,
and obtain the crown triumphantly,
so help us too, in our shared experience,
to see the goal of health and happiness,
rest and renewal,
and to attain the same,
for Your sake,
according to Your great plan.

74. FINDING A WAY OUT OF DARKNESS

We pray, Lord, for light before darkness;
We pray, Lord, for light amidst darkness;
We pray, Lord, for light to banish darkness;
We pray, Lord, for light instead of darkness;
We pray, Lord, for light reducing darkness;
We pray, Lord, for light to follow darkness;

And most of all we pray, Lord, for light leading us out of darkness.
Give us, Lord, a spark, a match, a candle, a bulb, a torch,
a lantern, a beacon, and then a blaze of light:
light that can never be extinguished, the light of the Holy Spirit
in our lives.
    All through our lives.

75. EXCHANGING PARENT AND CHILD ROLES

O God: on many occasions, we cannot understand Divinity
without using the image of a human family
Father, Son, Mother, Daughter.

You have ordained that sometimes -
    brother should be father to sister;
    sister, mother to brother;
    daughter, mother to father;
    son, father to mother;
    husband, father to wife -
    and perhaps most often daughter,
    mother to her own mother,
    daughter-in-law, mother to her adopted mother-in-law.

In our own lives, make us tolerant of these roles
so changed within the space of years so few.
Help us never to resent advice and instruction kindly given.
So may we value the love and dedication that comes
through being related to each other.

76. LOOKING FOR NEW PLEASURES

Basketwork, needlework, metalwork, woodwork;
Satellite, cable, digital, stereo;
Genealogy, sociology, archaeology, etymology;
What will it be?

At each stage in our lives,
we need new interests and new pleasures -
new diversions, new directions a different perspective,
different glimpses of a different landing stage,
a different staging point on our journey.

Lord, help us to engage in whatever we enjoy,
and to enjoy whatever we are engaged in.

Thereby may we expand where otherwise we would contract,
and explore where otherwise we would retreat.

77. A PRAYER FOR THE REST OF THIS FAMILY

O God, we pray now for all members of our family (ies).
Whatever they are doing in the morning;
Whatever they are doing this evening.

We pray for their health, their happiness, their hopefulness.

We pray for responsibilities they have acquired,
    And responsibilities they have shed
    For employment they have entered,
    And employment from which they have retired
    For residences they have taken over,
    And residences they have left.

We pray especially for _____ and _____
who have faced enormous difficulties this past week (month).
Guard, guide, protect and preserve our family (ies) evermore.

78. A PRAYER FOR OUR NEIGHBOURS

O God our Preserver:
Part of our being indoors so long, so much of each day,
and each week, makes us more aware of our neighbours.

We know so authoritatively where they go in the day,
at what time of the day, which day, and when they return.

We know who visits them, when and for how long.

We know who delivers, who attends, and who is sent away.

We know something of their moods and interests,
their choice of clothing and schooling.

Lifting curtains becomes quite addictive
chasing shadows, listening to distant voices.
We know that sometimes it is easier to understand many things
about a few families, rather than little about many families.
Grant these our neighbours fulfilment of all their aspirations.

79. THANK YOU FOR TOGETHERNESS
O God, our God,
Thank you for togetherness.
And thank you for each other.

Thank you for love, and loving kindness;
for grace and graciousness, for joy and joyfulness.

Thank you for humour - and our ability to overcome ill-humour;
for optimism - and our ability to defeat gloom and despondency.

Thank you for
    each other's strengths,
    each other's talents,
    each other's sympathies
for
    mistakes readily forgiven,
    hasty words readily forgotten - and
    indulgences readily accommodated.
Let us rejoice in a relationship some would call uneventful.
Deepen, broaden and lengthen that relationship, as we pray.

80. PREPARING TO PART
Lord: we are now preparing to part.

That makes us very sad, very tearful, very apprehensive.

There was always the possibility -
and latterly the probability - that this would happen,
but we always managed to push it to the back of our minds.

Now the time has arrived.

Be near to comfort and console us.

And in the midst of present uncertainty,
grant us the certainty that we shall be re-united
if not in a few weeks' time - then in Heaven.

SECTION 9: LOOKING AROUND

81. A PRAYER FOR OTHER CARERS

O God, sometimes I am so immersed in my own caring task
that I forget all others called upon to look after people who are
unwell or unfortunate, elderly <u>or</u> disabled, elderly <u>and</u> disabled.

These other carers also deserve my prayers.

I pray that they too might discover the faith
that I discovered when I did not see a way forward;
the strength that strengthened me when I felt so weak and frail;
the will that willed me when I might have given up;
the patience that eluded me when I became so edgy
and impatient.
Finally: I pray that these carers might find no demand too demanding,
no burden too burdensome,
no sacrifice too sacrificial.

82. A PRAYER FOR PEOPLE WITH NO CARING RESPONSIBILITIES

Lord, I pray for people with no caring responsibilities:
>   those who can laugh and play;
>   those who can go shopping and on holiday;
>   those who can visit library and concert hall;
>   those who can relax, knowing they are not on call.

I pray for these care-free individuals and families
that they might enjoy each hour and each day -
using each day for refreshment and renewal,
ready for the time when assuredly they will take up
and carry caring responsibilities of their own.

Build up their resources for these new demands
on their energies and imagination.

Equally, let me never be consumed by envy or bitterness.

Perhaps my moments of freedom are more precious
because they are fewer.

83. A PRAYER FOR THOSE EMPLOYED AS SOCIAL WORKERS
Lord, I pray for those employed as social workers
in their daily response to other people's crises.

Make them:
> fair, and firm;
> determined and disciplined;
> consistent and conscientious.

Save them from apathy, cynicism and indifference.
Save them from cutting costs rather than cutting misery.
Save them from writing so much that they visit so little.
And save them from the arrogance that they command
all the world's problems and all the world's solutions.

Eventually, Lord, make this our community so caring
that the "care in the community" that social workers teach
and preach might move from dream into reality.
> For Your Sake, To Your Glory.

84. A PRAYER FOR OCCUPATIONAL THERAPISTS
Like in Your great temples of old;
> they come for to measure;
> they come to gain new access;
> they come to lift great loads;
> they come to pull down some walls;
> and to raise other walls;
> they come to bring fresh supplies of water;
> they come with reels and rods and ramps,
> with seats that we might sit more upright,
> and beds that we might sleep more soundly.

These are our Occupational Therapists.

I pray for them, surrounded by all their aids and adaptations,
that they might give immobile people more mobility,
incapacitated people, greater capacity.

85. A PRAYER FOR A CARER'S PARTNER;
Lord, it is so difficult for _____

to see his (her) partner going through such agony, discomfort
and enforced idleness.

(S)he looks back to happier days
when both of them were fitter, fresher, freer to travel,
restricted only by children and money from travelling even further;

when both could see each other as true equals;
when both could think and plan a way ahead;
when both could take up new interests each new season.

(S)he now wakes up to gloomier days
when both face separation, impoverishment, and weariness.

Bless _____ in his (her) caring and sharing -
that it might be more than merely surviving,
rather the reviving of all past enthusiasms.

86. LOOKING FOR NEW METHODS OF CARING
Lord, I am stuck in my ways.

I try one routine to the neglect of other routines;
    one recipe - to the neglect of more varied recipes;
    one programme - to the neglect of better programmes;
    one armchair - to the neglect of cosier armchairs.

Each day, each week is perfectly predictable -
because it runs on tramlines.

Lord, take me beyond my set ways;
entice me out of entrenched habits;
make me question cherished customs.

May I never scorn other people's advice,
other people's methods, other people's secrets.

Instead, may I become brisker and bolder in all I undertake.

87 LOOKING FOR A PERMANENT SOLUTION TO SUFFERING

O God so often do I ask WHY?
> WHY the suffering?
> WHY the pain?
> WHY the misery?
> WHY the disease?

So often do I sow that another might reap;
I endure that another might prosper;
I labour that another might repose;
I wrestle that another might simply watch.

There is a land:
> a land flowing with milk and honey;
> a land where the sun rises and never sets;
> a land, yet undiscovered,
> where people ask what they might do for society -
> not what society might do for them.

Come. Come to meet me Jesus.
Rise from this tomb of suffering encasing humankind -
as surely as, in those days of old, You rose from Joseph's tomb.

88. LOOKING FOR ALTERNATIVE MEDICINES, ALTERNATIVE TREATMENTS

Dear God;
We know that most doctors and most nurses,
most patients and most carers,
expect familiar medicines, familiar treatments....
proven ways to combat illness, to combat pain.
But never shut our eyes to new medicines and new treatments;
new ways to ease the paralysis that impedes life;
or to reduce the fear that precedes death.

Renew in us an understanding of the miraculous: the miracle that can banish an allergy or reverse a coma; the miracle that can wither a tumour or restore lost eyesight.

So help us to understand more about mind over body -
just as Jesus first removed guilt and stress and unbelief
before curing many infirmities, performing many impossibilities.
Help us to re-discover Jesus where pills or physicians fail us;
to see the hand of Jesus in the many new, and unlikely,
agents of healing now within reach of our faith and hope.

---

89. LOOKING FOR WHAT IS SANITY AND INSANITY
O God:
What is sanity – and how shall it be recognised?

When we were disorientated, You gave us our bearings;
When we were fearful, You gave us courage;
When we were wakeful, You gave us slumber;
When we were doleful, You lifted our spirits.

Yet there are so many people muddled, terrified, restless
and depressed: people moving ever nearer the abyss of insanity.

What is insanity – and how shall it be recognised?

When our family and friends are beside themselves,
    help us to restore a right mind within them;
When our family and friends are nervous,
    help us to calm their nerves;
When our family and friends are volatile,
    help us to settle them down;
And when our family and friends despise and punish themselves,
    help us to draw them back to the safety of Your presence.

90. LOOKING AT DEVELOPING NATIONS WHICH HAVE FEWER CARERS
I am very aware that I live – and care –
In a country that actively promotes health and welfare;
a community with a safety net – set at many levels –
through which relatively few needy people can fall,
or fall a long way without alerting the rest of us.

> > >

I think today about countries still underdeveloped –
    with a shortage of medicines,
    with a shortage of nurses,
    with a shortage of doctors,
    with a shortage of hospitals
    and a shortage of places to go after hospital.

In these countries, there are fewer social workers, fewer priests,
fewer volunteers, and fewer carers outside the immediate family.
Yet may disabled people in these growing countries
somehow be supplied with new health and strength:
free from the fear that they will be displaced,
forgotten or abandoned - as much by wealthy developed
nations as by their own rulers.

SECTION 10: LOOKING FORWARD

91. A NEW SENSE OF PURPOSE

Through my solid door-frame, I see a tiny strip of light;

Through the hole in that fence, I see a tiny sprig of foliage;

Through dark clouds, I see a tiny hint of sunshine;

Through dusty dunes, I see a tiny drop of moisture.

My purpose here below seems to be giving,
and giving, and giving again until I can give no more.

Sometimes, Lord, the track round which I run
is merely circular. So soon, I am back where I started.

At these times I would more easily understand kindnesses
shown to me than my need to be kind,
benefits beneficial to me than my need to be benificent.

Renew my sense of purpose with the renewal of each day – and
may each eventide suggest new purpose for the day that follows.

92. A NEW PERSON TO CARE FOR
O Lord,

I now have _____ to care for.
This is exciting, challenging, extending.
Perhaps neither of us expected this opening, this opportunity.
Perhaps both of us would, some time, have quivered at the prospect.

Now give me patience and dedication, understanding and compassion.

And when these are in short supply
fill me with life anew.
May Your Holy Spirit replenish my resources, redouble my efforts.

93. A NEW CARE SETTING
O God,
I now have a new care setting

The walls are painted;
The beds are made;
The towels are unpacked;
The medicine cabinet is unlocked;
The pantry is full.

In this our new venture,
save us from being weighed down by old habits,
old methods,
old disagreements,
old reasoning.

Your angel has spoken:
"Behold, I make all things new."

If one single day for one single person is new,
then I know I have understood these words -
even as I have been understood.

94. A NEW SET OF COLLEAGUES
O God, our Provider:
Who sent Jesus to teach and to heal: not alone
but with two disciples, then four, then five, then twelve –
Eventually seventy-two -
Enlarge and enliven my task with a willing band of helpers,
that even as two score nurses are looking after four score patients
with twelve more resting - and sixty training -
so we may accomplish that which at first seemed beyond us,
and reach beyond that which we have already accomplished.

95. A NEW YEAR OF CARING

Another Year is Dawning
Dear Master, Let it be
In Working - or in Waiting,
Another Year for Thee.
> Another year, Lord:
> Another year of caring:
> caring for just one person, or for many people.
> Another year for forgetting myself:
> for drawing out the otherness within myself.
> Another year for receiving just a little thanks,
> but a lot of criticism.
> Another year of smiling through my tears:
> smiling <u>despite</u> my tears.
> Help me still to look forward to a fulfilled future
> without hankering after a care-free past.
> Another year, Lord.

Another Year of Progress;
Another Year of Praise;
Another Year of Proving;
Thy Presence all the Days.

(after Frances Ridley Havergal)

96. WAITING FOR MORE INFORMATION

I sit and wait for more information.
I phoned - but nobody told me who best to answer my phonecall.
I referred - but nobody told me who best to deal with my referral.
I joined a support group - but nobody told me
> how I might be best supported.

I read a booklet - but nobody told me whether this was the
> best booklet for me.

I asked for treatment - but nobody told me the best course of treatment.
I desperately want this new information - to become a better carer.
Some things I have kept doing, I should now cease doing;
And some questions I have kept avoiding, I should now confront.

97. WAITING FOR NEW INSPIRATION
Lord, I got up this morning determined to try harder:
> determined to be kinder,
> determined to be more patient,
> determined to be more attentive.

Yet - within an hour or two - I was
> just as irritable,
> just as cheerless,
> just as clueless,
> just as inflexible,
> as yesterday, and the day before.

I need to search my soul
Am I the wrong person in the wrong place at the wrong time?
Do I need a new burst of inspiration - like a billowing breeze to carry me further along?
Could that breeze blow through the dusty recesses of my life to clean out all mustiness and fustiness?
Could that breeze turn round this small craft, now becalmed?

98. WAITING FOR VERIFICATION
If this is the scan I've waited for:
> what will be its findings?

If this is the drug I've waited for:
> what will be its effects?

If this is the exploratory surgery I've waited for:
> what will be discovered?

If this is the diagnosis:
> what will be the symptoms?

If this is the prognosis:
> what will be the progression?

We might not want the truth.
We might not live comfortably with the truth.
We might distort the truth - till it becomes a different truth.
Yet, imperatively – imperceptibly - the truth shall set us free.

99. WAITING FOR MARCHING ORDERS
"They also serve who only stand and wait."

O God, I wait now to begin (to resume) caring.

The hospital will soon ring.

The ambulance (the cab) will soon be on its way.

A brief - and tantalising - time of rest and respite will be over.

The task of caring will soon consume most of my waking hours:
occupying most of my waking thoughts -
even when I am not actually on call.

I've been rather ill-at-ease these past few days:
always a bit apprehensive, unsure exactly what I have taken on.
Perhaps I have not been able to concentrate on myself:
least so, on myself.

Help me always to remember:
"They also serve who only stand and wait."

100. WAITING FOR MORNING
Keep, oh keep me
in Your care -
All through the night.

Keep, oh keep me
from despair -
All through the night.

Save, oh save me
from self-blame -
All through the night.

> > >

Save, oh save me
from dull shame -
All through the night.

Pray my restlessness should cease:
All through this night.

Pray my aching heart find peace:
All through this night.

Still glorifying God the Father; still glorifying God the Son;
Still glorifying God's Holy Spirit: At the end of this night.

CONCLUSION

However conscientious and dedicated a carer you are, or you become when called upon, there comes the moment to let go.

Your own health, physical or mental, might give way.

Carers' organisations have found that full-time carers suffer far more stress and far more ailments than other fully occupied people, paid or unpaid.

Or else the person(s) you are caring for might suffer declining health from an already low base. Comes the time when your charge must go into hospital or into long-term residential care, it is easy to feel guilt and failure.

When the person(s) you care for dies you are straight away made redundant. You probably receive no thanks and very little recognition for years or decades of selfless service. Other people avoid you in case death is catching, or for fear that you will go into enormous detail about your grief and loss.

Remember, loss is not diminished for being expected. Decline and death are often sudden even within the context of a long illness. We always tend to believe in better outcomes.

Sometimes the finishing, or the interruption, of a caring career comes when other members of the wider family make their demands known, or when they themselves need intensive care for a short or longer period.

In a society where 50 year-olds look after the 30 year-olds, and 10 year olds, how do the 70 year-olds cope with caring for the 90 year-olds, when those 70 year-olds too will soon be entitled to more attention? It is not uncommon for an 80 year-old to be looking after a centenarian parent whilst her own children are busy providing free child-care for their daughters and daughters-in-law.

Divorce, or a welcome return to full-time secular employment can be other interruptions to the caring cycle, as can homelessness (repossession), or a move to a different part of the country, to fit in with a spouse's employment.

Whatever the cause, ending care is a worrying and even guilt-ridden time.

Try not to see yourself as a failure, even when health professionals and unsympathetic relatives unwittingly imply that you have failed the person(s) you set out to care for.

Take the break in your caring to God in prayer. Do not hurry to resume caring straightway for someone else in need.

There will always be more people needing one-to-one attention than there are potential volunteers or conscripts. It could be God needs you for a completely different job; one which might only be of indirect benefit to the rest of society.

If you are talking to somebody who is a carer, when you are not, do not "beat round the bush." Most carers really want to talk about drawbacks and obstacles in their task, as with more neutral tasks. They definitely need to "ventilate." They frequently want "permission" to be angry and forthright. Moreover, they do not mind talking about illness and death.

One word of caution: never talk down to, or across, or above the head of the person(s) being cared for. They did not lose their emotions, or intelligence, their belief system or their ambitions when their health deteriorated. Travel with them.

✠

SUGGESTIONS FOR FURTHER READING

A large number of books are available covering the relationship between faith and healing. Also, very many <u>general</u> books of prayers contain prayers specifically for those who are suffering, and those who are concerned about their dependants young and old.

I have therefore selected here just a few titles which I have found meaningful. A glance along the shelves of any religious bookshop should reveal many more worth delving into.

Any titles now out-of-print are easy to track down in good second-hand bookshops.

THE OXFORD BOOK OF PRAYER
Ed. George Appleton, OUP, 1985.

THE LION PRAYER COLLECTION
Ed. Mary Batchelor, Lion, 1992.

THE S.P.C.K. BOOK OF CHRISTIAN PRAYER, SPCK, 1997.

EVERYDAY PRAYERS, Allen Birtwhistle, IBRA, 1978.

PRAYERS FOR HELP AND HEALING,
William Barclay, Fontana, 1968.

A WOMAN'S BOOK OF PRAYERS,
Rita Snowden, Fontana, 1968.

DAILY PRAYER,
Eric Milner-White & G.W. Briggs, Pelican, 1963

PRAYING FOR PEOPLE, Margaret Pawley, Triangle, 1992.

I'VE GOT TO TALK TO SOMEBODY, GOD.
Marjorie Holmes, Hodder, 1998.

POWER LINES: Celtic Prayers About Work,
David Adams, Triangle, 1992.

ROUGH WAYS IN PRAYER,
Paul Wallis, Triangle, 1995.

HEAVEN & CHARING CROSS, Edmund Banyard, NCEE, 1996.

SEASONS OF LIFE – Methodist Publishing House, 1997.

100 MEDITATIONS ON HOPE, Upper Room, 1995.

GAZING ON TRUTH: Meditations on Reality,
Kitty Muggeridge, Triangle, 1985.

FROM PAIN INTO PRAYER, Angela Ashwin, Fount, 1990.

EMBRACING GOD'S WORLD, Joyce Huggett, Hodder, 1996.

CHRISTIAN HEALING, Peter H. Lawrence, Terra Nova, 1997.

THE MEANING OF SERVICE, H.E. Fosdick, S.C.M., 1921.

HOPE WHEN YOU'RE HURTING, Dan Allender, Kingsway, 1997.

SPIRITUALITY & AGEING, ed. Albert Jewell, J. Kingsley, 1997.

ARE YOU LISTENING? Nick Fawcett, K.Mayhew, 1998.

COPING WITH ANXIETY & DEPRESSION,
Shirley Trickett, Sheldon, 1997.

HEALTH, HEALING AND WHOLENESS,
Howard Booth, A. James, 1998.

WERE YOU THERE? Rosemary Hartill, Triangle, 1995.

GOOD ENOUGH FOR GOD, Anne Townsend, Triangle, 1996.

CARING FOR YOUR ELDERLY PARENT,
Julia Burton-Jones, Sheldon, 1996.

USEFUL CONTACT POINTS

THE CARERS' NATIONAL ASSOCIATION
Write to: 20-25 Glasshouse Yard, LONDON EC1A 4JS.

    Helpline Number: 0345 573369
    Monday to Friday, 10am to Noon, 2pm to 4pm
    Calls are charged at local rates

AGE CONCERN
Write to: FREEPOST (SWB 30375) ASHBURTON, Devon TQ13 7ZZ.

    Helpline Number: FREEPHONE 0800 731 4931
    Monday to Friday, 9-30am to 5pm.

THE PRINCESS ROYAL TRUST FOR CARERS
    Tel: 0171 480 7788

CROSSROADS CARING FOR CARERS
    Tel: 01788 573653

ALZHEIMER'S DISEASE SOCIETY
    Helpline: 0845 300 0336
    Monday to Friday, 8am to 6pm

THE RELATIVES' ASSOCIATION
    (for relatives and friends of residents in elderly persons' homes)
    Tel: 0171 916 6055

THE ADMIRAL NURSE SERVICE
    (for families of people suffering dementia)
    Tel: 0171 636 8703

MACMILLAN CANCER RELIEF (the Macmillan Nurses)
    Tel: 0845 601 6161

MARIE CURIE CANCER CARE
Write (with SAE to 17 Grosvenor Crescent, London S141X 7XZ
    Tel: 0171 235 3325 or ring your local SOCIAL SERVICES

CARERS CHRISTIAN FELLOWSHIP
$^c/_o$ Chris & Brenda Baalham
14 Yealand Drive
Ulverston, Cumbria
LA12 9JB
Tel: 01229 585974

THE SAMARITANS
Head Office: 10 The Grove, Slough, Buckinghamshire SL1 1QP
Tel: 01753 216500.
There is a branch in every city, and most towns *(please see local directory)*

MOORLEY'S are growing Publishers, adding several new titles to our list each year. We also undertake private publications and commissioned works.

Our range of publications includes:
- **Books of Verse**
  - Devotional Poetry
  - Recitations
- **Drama**
  - Bible Plays
  - Sketches
  - Nativity Plays
  - Passiontide Plays
  - Easter Plays
  - Demonstrations
- **Resource Books**
  - Assembly Material
  - Songs & Musicals
  - Children's Addresses
  - Prayers & Graces
  - Daily Readings
  - Books for Speakers
- **Activity Books**
  - Quizzes
  - Puzzles
  - Painting Books
- **Daily Readings**
- **Church Stationery**
  - Notice Books
  - Cradle Rolls
  - Hymn Board Numbers

Please send a S.A.E. (approx 9" x 6") for the current catalogue or consult your local Christian Bookshop who should stock or be able to order our titles.